MW01264188

Making Sense
of Senselessness

Teri Kwal Gamble
College of New Rochelle

Michael W. Gamble
New York Institute of Technology

Boston   Burr Ridge, IL   Dubuque, IA   Madison, WI   New York   San Francisco   St. Louis
Bangkok   Bogotá   Caracas   Kuala Lumpur   Lisbon   London   Madrid   Mexico City
Milan   Montreal   New Delhi   Santiago   Seoul   Singapore   Sydney   Taipei   Toronto

McGraw-Hill Higher Education

A Division of The McGraw-Hill Companies

MAKING SENSE OF SENSELESSNESS
Teri Kwal Gamble, Michael W. Gamble

Published by McGraw-Hill, an imprint of The McGraw-Hill Companies, Inc.,
1221 Avenue of the Americas, New York, NY 10020. Copyright
© 2002 by The McGraw-Hill Companies, Inc. All rights reserved.

1 2 3 4 5 6 7 8 9 0 DOC/DOC 0 9 8 7 6 5 4 3 2 1

ISBN 0-07-283491-9

www.mhhe.com

TABLE OF CONTENTS

Foreword

September 11, 2001

The story of September 11, 2001 will be with us for a very long time. When we are asked about it years in the future, we will all remember where we were and what we were doing on September 11, 2001 when we first heard the news. The day is embedded in our mind. We watched it unfold. It is a day that had us witnessing jets turned into missiles. It is a day on which we watched people jumping singly or hand-in-hand out of the burning infernos. It is a day that will live as much in infamy as when Pearl Harbor was attacked. It is the day terrorism struck America brazenly and with a destructive force that its citizens had never witnessed so "up close and personal" before. It is the day on which more people died in America than on any other day since the Civil War. We thought what occurred was not possible, but it was. The Twin Towers of the World Trade Center and the Pentagon, monuments to capitalism and power, were attacked by enemies who believed that the buildings defined who we were and what we stood for.

Since 9/11/01, many people no longer feel as powerful or safe as they did on September 10, 2001. Terrorism triggered anxiety, fear, and anger. Since 9/11/01 heroism and patriotism have swelled. It may well be that September 11, 2001 has changed everything forever.

Now that time has passed, we offer this resource as a way to help make some sense out of that senseless day. It is an effort whereby we use communication principles to develop some clarity as we process the results of the day's events and seek to learn from them. Ours is a time to think, not to hate. Many of us are evaluating our priorities. We are facing a defining moment. We are taking time to look at ourselves and ask: "What will we make of it?" We hope these exercises help you answer that question. We hope they help you understand how and why communication works.

How to Use This Resource

Making Sense of Senselessness is a special collection of activities and exercises that pay tribute to 9/11/01. The exercises and activities have built-in flexibility. They can be approached in any order; we have grouped them according to the basic communication course for categorization purposes only. This volume is designed to help you explore a range of perspectives about terrorism and violence, as well as to re-evaluate your place in the world.

The activities and exercises interweave defining moments into the curriculum. They call on you to reflect on and research recent events. Some require you to use technology to find information, asking you to seek out background data on persons and/or events that are unfamiliar to you. Others require that you listen to those around you and suspend judgment. Still others request you to focus on what you are doing and feeling now as well as the kind of world you perceive yourself to live in today and hope to live in tomorrow.

Your instructors may guide you in using this resource, picking and choosing those exercises and activities that best fit the needs of your particular class. Or, you may be asked to work your way through this volume on your own. The fact is that although this resource was designed to meet the needs of communication classes and was prepared as a supplement to our book *Communication Works*, it can be used to enhance the study of other subjects such as English, Philosophy, Psychology, Sociology, Art, History, and Political Science. In addition, every exercise and activity can be used independently for personal development.

PART ONE

9/11/01 AND THE ESSENTIALS OF COMMUNICATION

Letter to Myself

Events and their contexts shape our communication experiences. So does one's personal need for affection, inclusion, and control. This exercise gives you a chance to consider how factors such as these influenced your reactions to the events of 9/11/01. The exercise calls on you to synthesize the responses you had on that day.

Prior to September 11, 2001, the major concern of many college students was their future careers. In addition, no central issue ignited everyone. Post September 11, 2001, college students are displaying a surging interest in global affairs and ethical issues.

In a letter or e-mail writing to yourself, describe how the events of September 11, 2001 affected your daily life. Be specific about your own reactions to the day's events including how and if you sought to give and receive comfort. Also describe the efforts you have made, if any, to regain ordinary life since then.

Seeing You, Seeing Me: Across Cultures

Culture influences communication. It tells us who we are, and how to behave. Ethnocentrism, the tendency to see our own culture as superior to all others, is a key characteristic of failed efforts at intercultural communication. On the other hand, cultural relativism enables us to try and understand the behavior of other groups based on the context in which the behavior occurs rather than solely from our frame of reference. Keeping this in mind, consider the following:

1. Surf the web and look at newspapers from Asia, the Middle East, and Europe to determine what they wrote about the events of 9/11/01 and the resulting worldwide conflicts. What does the information you discovered reveal about each region's perspectives on the terrorist attack, the subsequent war in Afghanistan, and about the people of the United States?

2. Explore the reasons why some Arabic women observe purdah or hijab (covering) and wear burqas (colored fabric that covers everything except a women's eyes) and chadors (large shawls).

3. The Pashtuns, a tribal society, are Afghanistan's dominant ethnic group to which much of the Taliban belong. In an effort to understand their culture, research the code of conduct Pashtuns adhere to.

4. According to Rudyard Kipling's *Kim*, "Certain things are not known to those who eat with forks." In your opinion, what is it we do not understand about terrorists and the Taliban? How could acquiring the knowledge we lack better equip us to counter both their physical and propagandistic attacks? In your opinion, what is it we do not understand

about Arabic culture? How could acquiring the knowledge we lack better equip us to communicate with Muslims?

5.   View one or more of the following films: *The Siege, True Lies, Rules of Engagement, Executive Decision,* and *Not Without My Daughter.* In what ways, if any, do these films perpetuate bias against Arabs?

6.   Finally, what is it like to feel different in your own country? After 9/11/01, some Muslim women felt the need to leave their head scarves at home out of fear for their personal safety. In an effort to demonstrate that there was no need to compromise the right to choose what is worn to support one's religious beliefs, some non-Muslim women donned scarves as a sign of solidarity with the Muslim women. How would wearing such a hijab make you feel? Would you do it to support the rights of others? Why or why not?

It's Artifactual

*We all communicate nonverbally. Nonverbal cues
provide us with "ways of knowing" that words alone do
not offer. Artifactual communication, the use of personal
adornment, is one kind of nonverbal communication that
has attracted special attention since 9/11/01. While some
oppose wearing the flag as clothing, others champion it.
This exercise calls on you to decide where you stand when
it comes to flag-based displays and why.*

The events of 9/11/01 precipitated both the wearing of
artifacts and the use of symbols as a means of displaying
and signaling patriotism. The question is, however,
whether such artifacts and symbols should have been used
by newspersons during newscasts. What do you think?

1. In your opinion, what messages were sent by
Americans who wore flag pins, wrapped themselves in
flag adorned clothing, placed flag decals on their cars, and
hung flags from their homes and places of business?

2. In your opinion, is it appropriate for a business owner
to hang a flag in order to attract patrons to his or her
establishment? Explain your answer.

3. In your opinion, is it appropriate for members of the
press to wear flag pins and display the flag during hard
news broadcasts? Interview programs? Entertainment
programs? Explain each of your responses.

The Mind-Body Connection

Communication with others can affect our health. When we are stressed and cut off from human contact, we put our health in jeopardy. Keep this fact in mind as you approach this exercise.

In John O'Neill's column "Vital Signs," ("Facing Up to Helplessness," *The New York Times,* November 6, 2001, F8) we learn that while investigating how stressful events affect the body, researchers determined that when subjects were passively subjected to upsetting scenes about which they could do nothing—such as the unending replays of the collapse of the World Trade Center, to which we were all exposed during the week of 9/11/01—the immune system could be undermined. In contrast, the immune systems of persons who were able to become active participants in a stressful activity remained healthy.

Armed with this background information, identify steps we might take to reduce the sense of helplessness precipitated in many of us by both the terrorist attacks of 9/11/01, and the subsequent anthrax attacks.

Male and Female Reactions

The way women and men use nonverbal communication often reflects societal practices. With this in mind, consider the following:

1. In the November 2001 issue of *Esquire Magazine*, in the article "War Comes to America," (p. 107-113), one of the featured writers, Scott Anderson, notes:

"It's an odd thing, probably not what one would predict or remember afterward, but when a person encounters true horror, the body's first response almost always occurs in the hands. With women, the hands tend to immediately come up to cover the mouth or press the cheeks. Among men, they tend to form a steeple over the nose and mouth or to clutch tightly onto the sides of the head. It is as if, in this moment of utter incomprehension and helplessness, the hands are trying to give comfort."

How else have the reactions of men and women to the events of 9/11/01 differed? In what ways have they been similar?

2. The effects of 9/11/01 provided us with visual images of men crying before the camera. Among them were Howard Lutnick, the CEO of Cantor Fitzgerald, CBS news anchor Dan Rather, Bernard B. Kerik, the New York City Police Commissioner, and Thomas Von Essen, the New York City Fire Commissioner. Compare press and public reactions to their tears with the reactions in 1972 to Senator Edmund Muskie of Maine, then a frontrunner among Democratic presidential candidates, who publicly wept at a press conference after denouncing a news editorial critical of his wife.

Finally, answer these questions:

    a.   Has our attitude toward men's tears changed over the past few decades? If so, how do you account for the change?

    b.   Review the following two books in an effort to explain if we no longer view tears as a sign of weakness: Glenn Hendler, *"Sentimental Men: Masculinity and Politics of Affect in American Culture,"* University of California, 1999, and Tom Lutz, *"Crying: The Natural and Cultural History of Tears,"* Norton, 2001.

    c.   In your opinion, why, if men are being released from tearlessness, do many still expect female leaders to cry?

Images of Women and Men

Beliefs about gender-appropriate behavior may differ from culture to culture. Among the variables used to distinguish cultures are individualism vs. collectivism, high-context vs. low-context communication, and high-power distance vs. low-power distance. Individualistic cultures stress individual goals, while collectivistic cultures stress group goals. High-context cultures encourage indirectness in communication, while low-context communication cultures encourage directness. In high-power distance cultures, subordinates defer to superiors, while in low-power distance cultures power is used only when legitimate. Keep these distinctions in mind as you approach this exercise.

After the Western Alliance recaptured Kabul from the Taliban, images of Afghan women removing their burkas and revealing their faces in public for the first time in years flooded the airwaves. While Afghan women used their newly restored freedom to let the sun shine on their faces and show flecks of their hair, Afghan men now also used their newly felt freedom to shave their faces of the beards, at least four inches long, that they had been forced to wear by the Taliban. In addition, they bought CD's, DVD's, television sets, and pin-ups of beautiful girls, while women's purchases of burkas ceased. Writing in her column entitled "Cleopatra and Osama," Maureen Dowd (*The New York Times,* November 18, 2001, WK 13) noted: "There have been many repressive regimes throughout history. But the Taliban were obsessively focused on denying gender, sexuality, and the forces at the very gut of life."

Counter pointed against these scenes was one playing itself out on American television. The ABC television network broadcast a first for television, both network and cable—the Victoria's Secret Fashion Show—featuring women parading in thong panties. According to Alex Kuczynski's article "Victoria's Secret on TV: Another First for Women,"

(*The New York Times,* Sunday, November 18, 2001, Section 9, p. 1) hundreds of callers registered complaints with the Federal Communications Commission about the program's airing.

Where do you stand? In your opinion is there a parallel between Muslim women shedding their burkas and showing their hair, and American women shedding their clothes and showing their skin? Could it be that both sets of women are dressing their certain ways because of what men want them to do?

To what extent, if any, do you believe that the Taliban's denying the gender and sexuality of women was a reflection of their hyper-, or insecure, masculinity?

To what extent, in your opinion, was the Victoria's Secret Fashion Show a reflection of women's hyper-, or insecure, femininity?

In your opinion, will the American practice of displaying hyper-sexualized images of women via the mass media become more or less acceptable now? Why?

10

Words and Their Post 9/11/01 Meanings

Since meaning is what communication is all about, by understanding how language works, we also understand how communicators use words to help create meanings and expectations. Keep this in mind as you answer the questions below. Also consider how the choice of words in each question affects your answer to the question.

1. Is *psychological torture* justified in order to jump-start the investigation of the worst crime in American history?

2. Is *court sanctioned psychological interrogation* justified in order to jump-start the investigation of the worst crime in American history?

(Be certain to assess the implications of the language used in questions 1 and 2. Ask yourself if the second question is just a politically correct restatement of the first question. Whether you determine that it is or is not, explain your reasons.)

3. Given the events of 9/11/01 and the Anthrax scare following it, how have the meanings you have for the words "handle with care" changed?

4. Identify and discuss any other words whose meanings you believe have changed since 9/11/01.

It's a Simile

A metaphor is a figure of speech that makes a direct identification between two things: "That woman is a butterfly," "My love is a flower." A simile is a figure of speech that compares two things not usually paired together and uses the words "like" or "as": "That man sits like a pretzel," "My love is like a rose." Both metaphors and similes tie a new idea to an idea with which the audience is already familiar. Whereas a metaphor suggests equivalence, a simile suggests similarity.

The following similes were used to describe the attack on the World Trade Center:

> Like Nagasaki
> Like "Independence Day"
> Like "The Towering Inferno"
> Like "The Siege"
> Like bad science fiction
> Like a Tom Clancy novel
> Like a bad dream

Using an original simile or other figure of speech of your own choosing, describe the World Trade Center attack from your perspective.

PART TWO

9/11/01 AND INTERPERSONAL COMMUNICATION

Letter to You

When we purposely reveal information to another person about ourselves, or our relationship with them, which that person wouldn't otherwise know, we engage in self-disclosure. The amount of disclosing we do with another person is a gauge of how close we feel to the person or how close we desire to become. How do you decide whether it is or is not appropriate for you to share your innermost thoughts, feelings, and intentions with others? Ask yourself this question as you approach this exercise.

As horrible as 9/11/01 was, it has made some of us think about our mortality and the possibility of losing those we love. With this in mind what would you want to tell your closest family members and friends about you and the feelings you have about them? How do you imagine that their knowing this information will affect the relationships you share with them?

Technology And The Effort to Preserve The Memories of Days of Terror And Tribute

Newer, emerging technologies are reshaping how we communicate and altering the nature of our communication experiences. In addition to giving us new ways of receiving information, they also give us new ways of relating to others. As you approach this exercise consider how technology is changing your communication landscape.

1. First, compare and contrast the nature and impact of messages received via traditional mail and e-mail. Then, answer the following question:

How do you believe that the events of September 11, 2001 and the subsequent anthrax threats will affect the future of both the United States Postal Service and E-mail?

2. For many people the ordeal of September 11, 2001 became an opportunity to make friends. For example, some Web sites offer testimony to the enduring friendships of passengers who were on some of the two hundred planes rerouted after the attack.

Log onto any of these Web sites

http://communities.msn.com/TheRefugeesofAirFranceFlight004

http://www.theganderconnection.org/index.html

http://www.ua929.org/

After describing their respective contents, how do you account for the forging of so many friendships during the crisis?

15

3. In an effort to deal with the events of 9/11/01, many people created personal Web pages and used them to vent anger, frustration, and sorrow by telling others how they felt. Some have alluded to this phenomenon as the "new talk radio"—meaning the sites functioned like a forum to release feelings with digital tools that enabled users to add audio, video, photographs, and links to others. Describe the content of a Web page that you would like to use to share your feelings about and memories of 9/11/01 with others.

4. Electronic artifacts like Web pages, E-mail and broadcast and cell signals tend to be more fleeting than the messages people commit to paper, which more easily preserve the past. In order to memorialize September 11, 2001, the San Francisco based Internet Archive project working with the Library of Congress has been making copies of Web sites since September 11, 2001. The project has amassed over 500 million pages from a few thousand sites. Americans have saved E-mail just as Americans two or more generations ago kept newspapers from the Pearl Harbor attack. In addition, TV broadcasts are being digitally stored. Verizon has also produced cassette tapes of the final voice-mail messages left by the terrorist attack's victims, and NPR is soliciting tapes from victim's families and others in order to create a snapshot of what people were thinking at a very critical time in this nation's history. You can explore some of the rescued memories on www.archive.org, www.televisionarchive.org, and www.webarchivist.org.

To add to the oral history being created, make a tape that recalls your impressions of the day.

16

Interpersonal Shifts

Every communication experience serves one or more functions. For example, communication can help us define who we are, enable us to establish meaningful relationships, or prompt us to examine and change our attitudes or the attitudes of others. Keep this in mind as you consider how the events of 9/11/01 influenced attitudes toward the importance of interpersonal connections.

1. Conduct research in an effort to determine:

   a. If and/or how the events of 9/11/01 impacted the marriage and divorce rates of your county or state.

   b. Whether people in your county or state are re-evaluating the choices they've made about jobs and career success.

2. After experiencing the events of 9/11/01 what aspects of your social and career life have you personally decided are and are not worth pursuing?

3. How did that day's events and the aftermath influence your attitudes regarding the importance of family and intimate bonds?

4. After 9/11/01, gay partners of those killed sought their share of federal survivor dollars. Do you believe Congress and the courts should recognize the legal relations of gay partners, treat them as family, and compensate them for their losses?

5. In your opinion, what role does fear play in helping persons realize their essential values?

6. Are you the type of person you think you wanted to be? Why or why not?

Heroes: Female and Male

We react to the messages we, and others, send. Feelings influence behavior. Expectations influence performance. With this in mind, this exercise asks you to consider how 9/11/01 influenced prevalent conceptions of masculinity and femininity.

1. According to some, on and since 9/11/01, our treatment of the firefighters, police, emergency personnel, and passengers of flight 93 who responded by overcoming the hijackers reveals that a new manliness is in vogue. In your opinion, what do the events of 9/11/01 tell us about how the male hero is being resurrected? Compare and contrast the image of the new male hero with:

> The masculinely-aggressive model
>
> The belief advanced by some that, due to technological advances, men no longer need physical strength
>
> The feminized male

Also, research press coverage of the perceived heroes of the day in an effort to count the number and nature of references to heroes, both male and female. Discuss the implications of your discoveries.

2. Define heroism. What psychological/behavioral characteristics do you believe differentiate heroes/rescuers from bystanders/observers? Compare and contrast the definition and characteristics you identified with those identified by heroism researchers.

Gender and Emotional Impact

There is a connection between gender and communication. People may communicate differently with you just because of your gender. Have you considered how gender influences the way you interpret experience including how you process the messages of others? This exercise calls on you to do that.

Working individually or in groups, compile a list of potential reasons you would use to account for the following survey research finding published in the November 17-23rd issue of *TV Guide* (p. 59).

When it comes to the emotional impact of TV news coverage of the events of 9/11/01, 18 percent of women find the news frightening as opposed to five percent who say it's reassuring. The numbers are practically reversed for men with seven percent saying it's frightening and 14 percent finding it reassuring.

PART THREE

9/11/01 AND COMMUNICATING IN THE SMALL GROUP

What Difference Does a Woman Make?

What are the consequences of treating persons differently because of their gender? Can a society's gender constructs limit the way persons are perceived and the opportunities afforded them? Keep these questions in mind as you respond to the questions below.

1. How do you imagine our culture would change if women were not featured in advertising, allowed to attend school, have a job outside the home, or participate in the political process?

2. What are the effects a country might realize if it were to push women out of educational, political, and economic spheres?

3. In your opinion, what does the practice of forced (not voluntary) veiling reveal about male attitudes toward women?

4. Research the extent to which the repression of women functions as a political tool for achieving and consolidating power.

5. Currently, the United States Selective Service registers for the draft all male citizens between the ages of 18 and 25 who could be used in the event of a national security crisis. Do you believe that the selective service should also register women aged 18 through 25? Why or why not?

6. According to M.G. Lord, the author of *Forever Barbie: The Unauthorized Biography of a Real Doll* (William Morrow, 1994), interest in purchasing military Barbie dolls, also popular after the Desert Storm Gulf War campaign of the 1990s, soared after 9/11/01. Lord notes, "Actually, you could look at Barbie as being important because she's the totem of everything

the terrorists who attacked us hate. . . she's the archetype of the single, undraped, super-sexualized American female, a woman who has a job and a boyfriend and is liberated." Do you agree? If so, why? If not, why not? In your opinion, should combat be a Barbie-doll mission?

What if There Were No Word for Terrorism?

The labels we use help shape the way we think, perceive the world, and behave. According to the Sapir-Whorf hypothesis, people from diverse cultures perceive events differently, at least in part, because of their language differences. Using this knowledge, assess the following situation and answer the questions that follow.

In November of 2001, the Army's Psychological Warfare Unit gathered in Fort Bragg, North Carolina to decide how best to explain the September 11th terrorist attacks on the World Trade Center and the Pentagon, together with the U.S. bombing of Afghanistan, to the millions of Afghans, many of whom had never seen a major city, let alone a skyscraper. Complicating their task was the realization that the Afghan languages of Dari or Pashto contained no word for terrorism.

Your task today is to participate in a brainstorming group whose task it is to help the Army. Your charge is the following:

How would you use leaflets featuring few if any words, radio, and loudspeakers to:

    1. persuade enemy fighters to quit, and

    2. convince civilians, many of whom are illiterate, that U.S. bombing will result in a better future for their families.

Once you devise your own plan to accomplish these objectives, evaluate these efforts reported by Greg Jaffe ("An Elite Army Team Opens a New Front: The Afghan Mind," *The Wall Street Journal*, November 8, 2001, A1, A6) that Psychological Operations actually put into operation.

1. One leaflet showed a Taliban soldier using a metal rod to beat several women, covered head to toe in their Islamic robes, called burqas: "Is this the future you want for your women and children?" it asked in both Dari and Pashto, the two most common Afghan languages.

2. The humanitarian food rations dropped by the United States were initially colored the same shade of yellow as cluster bombs and the markers used in mine fields. Ultimately, the ration's color were changed to light blue.

3. They broadcast music banned by the Taliban, together with references to the massive Buddha statues destroyed by the Taliban, and tips for surviving the bombing.

How Much Is One Life Worth?

In our society critical decisions are usually relegated to groups. Brainstorming is one technique groups use to promote thinking and decision-making. Use the technique as you tackle this problem. Also consider this: How does the fact that either you or the persons whom you know may have had friends or family members die as a result of the tragic events of 9/11/01 influence your decision-making?

Identify the criteria you would use in order to determine how much a jury should award the survivors of persons killed during the World Trade Center and Pentagon attacks. Don't hesitate to ask tough questions as you seek to complete this task. For example, while you may choose to compensate survivors for the pain and suffering of the victims, if the victims died instantly is there any suffering to compensate? Once you have completed your list of criteria, you may want to compare them with those identified in "A Lawyer's Worksheet" contained in William Glaberson's article, "Lawyer's Math in September 11 Deaths Shows Varying Values for Life," (*The New York Times,* November 11, 2001, B1, B10).

Surviving Terrorism

*When a group reaches a consensus, all members agree on
the decision. Consensus puts the resources of the entire
group to use. Your goal, after considering the question
below individually, is to reach a consensus by discussing
this situation with others.*

You are part of a task force charged with deciding what
items U.S. citizens need to have in order to survive the
worst. Your specific task is to identify those 10 items to
be included in a 72-hour emergency survival kit for one
person. Once you devise your list, compare and contrast
it with the list devised by experts as reported in Barbara
Carton's article "Apocalypse Now: Stocking Up to
Survive the Worst," (*The Wall Street Journal,*
Wednesday, October 10, 2001).

PART FOUR

9/11/01 AND COMMUNICATING TO THE PUBLIC

How Critical Is Thinking, Really?

Being able to think critically about controversial issues and speak cogently about them are skills essential to a democratic society. This exercise calls on you to use your critical thinking skills to answer the questions below.

1. Following 9/11/01, government officials and first amendment scholars were at odds over whether the speeches and comments of terrorist leader Osama bin Laden should be aired on television and radio newscasts or published in books and newspapers for all to hear and view. Debate also ensued over whether Americans and others should be able to view Web sites containing Al Qaeda recruitment films.

In your opinion, of what merit, if any, are a terrorist's words? Do you believe it is important to expose ourselves to content which we find objectionable or with which we disagree? Why or why not? Do you believe that censorship of the words of terrorists or war news undermines the public's trust? Why or why not? In any case, what behaviors ought we exhibit if we are to listen to and view such materials critically? Be specific.

2. During November 2001, approximately 2000 printed and CD copies of a book titled *Scientific Principles of Improvised Warfare and Home Defense Volume 6-1: Advanced Biological Weapons Design and Manufacture* were sold. Some refer to this book as a "a germ-warfare cookbook," (Paul Zielbauer with William J. Broad, "In Utah, a Government Hater Sells a Germ-Warfare Book," *The New York Times*, November 21, 2001, B1, B6) In your opinion, should books that offer readers the ability to build crude biological weapons, capable of killing thousands of people, be available for purchase? What if the information contained in the book is already available on the Internet or in military and biology books available in public libraries?

30

Protestors and the Web

*The Internet enables people around the world to
communicate with each other. As we expand our
communication repertoire, we also expand the numbers of
persons we are able to reach. Have you used the Internet
to find persons who share views similar to or different
from your own? Should you? Which group do you aspire
to reach the most? Why?*

   While certainly in the minority on this issue, not
everyone approved of President George W. Bush's
decision to bomb Afghanistan. News coverage of
opposition positions, however, was scant making it
difficult for anti-war activists to find and/or support each
other. Here, the Internet proved to be a powerful tool for
dissenters to find allies. In addition, by using the Web as
their mobilization headquarters, protestors were able to
accomplish a number of things. For example, they were
able to download leaflets to hand out at anti-war
demonstrations, gather electronic signatures for an online
peace petition presented to Prime Minister Tony Blair,
and express alternative points of view anonymously
thereby alleviating fear of reprisal for statements of
dissent. Thus, it might well be, that the Internet made it
possible for the minority to publish opinions that they
otherwise might have hesitated to express in public for
fear of isolating themselves simply because of their
unpopular views.

Conduct some research in an effort to determine the role
the Internet could play to decrease the effects of the Spiral
of Silence, a theory of communication developed by
Elisabeth Noelle-Neumann. How, for example, might the
Internet enable those who find themselves in the minority
on controversial issues to withstand the force of public
opinion?

Note: Among the Internet sites you might explore for
background information on the Spiral of Silence are:

http://oak.cats.ohiou.edu/~cw619696/spiral.htm

http://web.syr.edu/~mlgryszk/spiral.html

http://www.afirstlook.com/archive/spiral.cfm?source=arc

hther

Information Versus Propaganda

Given that an educated public is better able to make informed decisions, how important is it for all of us, including the members of the press, to have access to reliable information? Keep this question in mind as you complete the following activities:

1.   During the U.S. war against the Taliban, members of the U.S. media were given no direct access to military units on the ground or to the sites from which they had been launched. As a result, U.S. reporters were unable to provide much independent, first hand, observation. Given this situation, discuss the extent to which, if any, you believe the line between information and propaganda was blurred during both the Gulf and Afghan wars.

In your discussion, compare and contrast the access journalists had to information during both World War II and the Vietnam War with the access afforded them during the Gulf and Afghan wars.

How do you reconcile the media's mission to report the facts which can mean disclosing failures and foul-ups, with the military's mission to win the war (which can mean not giving the media what they want when they want it) and to avoid jeopardizing operations and endangering troops?

2. As U.S. bombing continued to make it possible for the Northern Alliance to recapture territory from the Taliban, President George W. Bush named the building that houses the Justice Department for the antiwar presidential candidate Robert F. Kennedy (who also had been the U.S. Attorney General). Just the day before, Kennedy's daughter, Kerry Kennedy Cuomo, had declared publicly that her father would never have supported the restrictions on civil liberties that the current President and Attorney General called for.

Conduct research in an effort to determine what civil liberties were restricted in the fight against terrorism and the potential impact that these restrictions might have on our privacy and freedom. In your opinion, does our need for security justify the restrictions? Are there any other ways that our security could be protected without the curtailment of these rights? Why or why not?

Both Sides Now

When speaking on a proposition of policy, the speaker's goals are to demonstrate a need for the policy and earn audience support for it. Attempt to fulfill both goals while working on this activity.

After September 11, 2001, the U.S. government suspended the writ of habeas corpus which required that an inmate be brought to the court so it could assess whether or not that person had been imprisoned lawfully and whether or not she or he should be released from custody. Instead, the government held thousands of detainees in secret, approved wiretaps on prisoners' conversations with their lawyers, and debated the advisability of using torture to make suspects talk.

Divide into pro (should be) and con (should not be) teams. Each team should choose one of the following propositions of policy to research and present a speech on:

1. The U.S. government should be (should not be) permitted to hold detainees in secret.

2. Wiretaps on prisoners' conversations with their lawyers should be (should not be) permitted.

3. Torture should be (should not be) used to make suspects talk.

The task of each pro and con speaker is to demonstrate a need for the position s/he is espousing on the subject policy.

In a brief paper, speakers should also identify the tools and tactics they used in their presentation in an effort to persuade receivers to accept the position they were taking. Similarly, receivers need to identify and report on any examples of flawed reasoning exhibited by the speakers.

Receivers should also be able to compare and contrast the effectiveness of the pro and con presentations as well as evaluate which of the pro speakers and which of the con speakers made the best case for their position with reasons for their choice.

Finally, both speakers and receivers should identify the moral and legal problems that are associated with the position taken.

The Fear Factor

Persuaders sometimes use fear appeals to accomplish their objectives. When using a fear appeal, the persuader describes a threat, suggests that receivers are likely to experience the threat, and indicates that receivers may avoid or diminish the threat by following the persuader's advice. In your opinion, when, if ever, is it appropriate for persons who are attempting to persuade others to think, believe, or do as they advocate, to use fear appeals? As you ponder this question, also consider this:

According to journalist Jonathan Alter, in his article "Time to Think About Torture," (*Newsweek,* November 5, 2001, p. 45), Jordanian investigators broke down a 1980s terrorist, Abu Nidal, by threatening his family. Similarly, according to Alter, Philippine police were able to help solve the 1993 World Trade Center bombing (plus a plot to crash 11 U.S. airliners and kill the Pope) by convincing a suspect that they were about to turn him over to the Israelis.

In your opinion, when it comes to solving crimes involving terrorism, what, if any, value are fear appeals? And, if in the U.S. we sanction the use of fear appeals in advertising (insurers, for example, ask: "What will happen to them when you are gone?") and political discourse (politicians warn: "If we don't allow you, the citizen, to invest your social security contributions in the stock market, the system could become insolvent as baby boomers retire") are we on firm footing to object to its use during criminal or terrorist interrogations?

Where Do You Stand? Then and Now

Audience analysis is important for anyone seeking to understand and/or influence the attitudes of receivers. A tool you can use to determine receiver attitudes is an opinion poll. Persuaders use polls to assess attitudes, to guide them in constructing messages designed to change attitudes, as well as to evaluate the effectiveness of messages sent in an effort to change or buttress attitudes.

Take a poll to determine if your peers supported U.S. actions in Afghanistan when they began in September of 2001.

Take a second poll to determine if they are supportive of U.S. policy today.

In your polling, try to identify the reasons that underlie the positions they are expressing.   Which, if any, of the messages they received led them to strengthen or change their position? Compare the results of your polls, with those reported by professional pollsters. Then answer these questions:

To what extent, if any, do results reveal a shared, cohesive body of public opinion and values?

Research the views held by those Americans who opposed the War in Afghanistan and admittedly were on the margin of mainstream opinion.

Anthrax Facts

Credibility is made up of three factors: trustworthiness, expertise, and dynamism. If receivers determine that a source is untrustworthy, incompetent, or passive, they are less likely to accept that source's message.

Conduct research in an effort to compare and contrast the communications the government had with the public about anthrax with those it communicated to the public about the West Nile Virus.

In your opinion, looking back at the sequence of events, what did the administration do or fail to do that precipitated or undermined public trust? To what extent, if at all, did officials follow these four guidelines for minimizing panic and helping people adapt to changing circumstances?

1. Adhere to a policy of full disclosure regarding what is and is not known and deliver this information in a non-patronizing manner.

2. Refrain from speculating and mixing facts with reassurance.

3. Provide a thorough account of what's being done to counter the threat.

4. Recommend specific steps that people may take to protect themselves.

Speech Support I and II

Attention getting devices, supporting materials, and audio and visual aids help a speaker flesh out ideas as well as stir receivers. Persuaders use such tools to enhance audience understanding and make their statements more believable.

1. President Bush delivered a number of speeches to the nation following the terrorist attacks of September 11, 2001. Pick one of his speeches and identify the kinds of attention getting and supporting devices the President used when he spoke to the American people and the world.

2. How could you use definitions, statistics, examples and illustrations, testimony, comparisons and contrasts, repetition and restatement, visual aids, audio aids to enhance a speech on one of the topics listed below?

> The Life Cycle of Anthrax
>
> How Humans are Infected with Anthrax
>
> The Types of Anthrax

Provide an example of each type of support you identify.

The War of Words

Gaining access to the marketplace of ideas, and being free to advocate ideas whether they are popular or unpopular, are essential qualities to the maintenance of a free society. Keep this in mind as you respond to the questions that follow.

1. During the war on terrorism that followed the terrorist attacks of 9/11/01, there was fear that because the press in various countries badly distorted the image of America, America would lose the battle of ideas within those countries that harbored terrorists. Given that none of the nations on the State Department's list of state sponsors of terrorism has an Internet usage rate of more than ten percent of its population, what steps do you believe America should take to better wage the war of words?

2. The war of words has another dimension. The American Council of Trustees and Alumni, a conservative nonprofit group devoted to curbing liberal tendencies in academia, compiled a list of statements they labeled as anti-American and accused those who made the statements of exhibiting unpatriotic behavior after September 11, 2001. A list of the statements was featured on the group's Web site (www.goacta.org/Reports/defciv.pdf). The group contends that such quotes are evidence that colleges and universities are failing America.

Among the quotations featured on the Web site are: "Build bridges and relationships, not simply bombs and walls," "Ignorance breeds hate," and "If Osama bin Laden is confirmed to be behind the attacks, the United States should bring him before an international tribunal on charges of crimes against humanity."

Other scholars who object to the list contend that the quotations on it were taken out of context and caution that the list itself "has a little of the whiff of McCarthyism," referring to McCarthy-era blacklisting.

Where do you stand? Should the advocacy of ideas be suppressed in a free society during times of crisis? In your opinion do ideas create potential hazards? Is freedom of speech only for ideas we agree with, or is its purpose to allow the expression of ideas with which we might not agree? Explain your position.

APPENDIX

9/11/01 AND
MASS COMMUNICATION
AND MEDIA

The Turning Point

As humans, we have the unique ability to reflect on ourselves, as well as on situations that we face. No matter what your current age or position, spending time considering who you are is extremely important, especially after experiencing a life-altering event. This exercise calls on you to develop a collage that links past, present, and future images of you and your world. It calls on you to predict those changes you imagine will occur as a result of 9/11/01.

According to authors William Strauss and Neil Howe ("September 11 Tragedy Marks Another Turning Point," *USA Today,* October 20, 2001, 15 A), history tells us that we enter a new era—a new turning—approximately every 20 years or so. At the inauguration of each turning, people change how they feel about themselves, the culture, the nation, and the future. According to Strauss and Howe, turnings come in cycles of four and span four generations.

The first turning spanned the years from VJ (Victory in Japan) day through the early 1960s.

The second turning is an "awakening" spanning the years from Kennedy's assassination through the early 1980s.

The third turning is an "unraveling" and takes us up to September 10, 2001.

The fourth turning is a "crisis" (beginning 9/11/01).

In order to consider the changes, which you may believe will result from of the events of 9/11/01, respond to these questions:

1. How will our civil liberties and sense of individualism be affected?

2. How will our current celebrity culture be affected?

3. Will our media feature less violent fare in the years ahead?

4. Will we become less global and more natavistic in focus?

5. How will aging Baby Boomers, Gen-Xers, and Millennials be affected?

6. How will the current fourth turning turn out?

The Ratings War

*Interpreting messages received from the media is
important to the well being of our society, as is being able
to identify the functions served by the media and the
means they use to perform these functions. Keeping this
in mind, answer the following questions either
individually or in groups.*

1. How have your attitudes toward the news, both print
and broadcast, changed since 9/11/01?

2. To what extent, if any, have the labels given post
9/11/01 newscasts such as "War on Terror," "Homeland
Security," and "Anthrax in America" affected how you
respond to the news?

3. What steps, if any, have you taken to selectively
control your news intake? Be specific.

4. How do you believe that competition between news
sources affected and is continuing to affect the nature of
the coverage given? In other words, what kind of
attention getting devices were and are being used by
competitors to arrest reader/viewer attention?

Advertising and War

The goal of persuasive discourse is to modify the thoughts, beliefs, or actions of a target audience. In order to realize such a goal, professional persuaders often seek to make receivers feel as well as think. Keep this in mind as you complete the next activity.

You are a newly appointed member of the Advertising Council, the group charged with creating U.S. public service ads supporting the war effort and raising morale. Back in 1942, the Advertising Council was called the "War Advertising Council". It created the now famous wartime campaigns "Rosie the Riveter" and "Loose Lips Sink Ships." After researching these campaigns, your goal is to identify what messages you would use to sell America's perspective on terrorism overseas— particularly in Muslim nations—to offset the negative messages that have been spread there.

Commemorating 9/11/01

In groups, decide what we should do each year on the anniversary of 9/11/01 in order to commemorate it. In other words, what can we do personally, in public, and using the media to mark that this was a day like no other?